CW00742669

How to mal
a difference by
transforming
managers into
leaders

Copyright © Go M.A.D. Ltd

First published in Great Britain in 2004 by

Go MAD Books
Pocket Gate Farm
Off Breakback Road
Woodhouse Eaves
Leicestershire
LE12 8RS
United Kingdom

All rights reserved. No part of this publication may be reproduced, stored in a retrieval system, or transmitted in any form or by means without prior consent of the publisher.

ISBN No. 978-0-9933414-3-4

ThinkOn® is a registered trademark and trading name of Go M.A.D. Ltd

Foreword

Welcome to our latest edition of this tips book on how to transform managers into leaders, containing over 300 thought provoking ideas to help you make a difference about your leadership.

The ThinkOn® system, that we use to underpin all our programmes across the world, is universally applicable to any topic. We've now firmly embedded this throughout the book so it's even easier to apply it to your leadership development.

We've updated it with some of our own thinking in recent years, in particular by enlarging the section on the ThinkOn® Leadership Framework. This means this book can now help your thinking as a team as well as at an individual level.

We've also made it even more practical for you, by adding at the end of each section, space for you to turn your ideas on leadership into action.

And with the help of some of our valued clients we have increased the number of tips to over 300.

What's stayed the same?

Whilst styles of leadership may have changed over the decades and the advance of technology and increase in remote and global working may have significantly shifted people's paradigm of what being at work means, leadership is still an enduring theme that stands the test of time. It is still something that you can take personal responsibility for every day. Raise your awareness of the choices you make as a leader and the impact of those choices on others.

The previous edition of this book contained 255 tips generated by leaders at a ThinkOn conference – those tips are still valid today and still in the book, so I'd like to thank all of those people who made an input then, as well as our new contributors for this edition. You are gratefully acknowledged at the end of this book.

Reading this book alone will not transform you into a leader. But the practical application of the ideas you read will get you started. Combine those ideas with the ThinkOn® system and you will increase your probability of success significantly.

Keep making a difference.

Andy Gilbert
Managing Director
Go MAD Thinking

Managers and Leaders – what is the difference?

So what is the difference between a 'Manager' and a 'Leader'? I will be quoting nothing new if I say 'Tasks are managed, people are led'. This very simple explanation says it all. Managers control resources, juggle, organise, administer them, but if people are 'controlled' they tend to rebel, not take responsibility for their own actions and lose the power to think for themselves. If you have a boss or have had a boss in the past, just spend a few moments to think about that person. The extent to which you enjoy working for this person and would go out of your way to go the extra mile for him or her is really a measure of their effectiveness as a leader. If, by contrast, you feel your boss is like 'Big Brother', controlling your every movement and treating you like a pawn in the chessboard of business, then that person is treating you exactly the same as any other resource, and is much more 'manager' than 'leader'. A leader, by definition, requires followers – real people who are inspired to climb onto the same bandwagon.

One of our contributors wrote: "The question is provocative and implies leaders are better than managers. Businesses need both managers and leaders." I don't deny this at all. I see a 'manager' as a position, and one that people might aspire to. Being a 'leader' is not a position, but is something a person is through their own actions and attitude. In business, not everyone can be a 'manager', but they are needed to manage resources and tasks. However, everyone can be a leader, whatever their position, whether receptionist or CEO – the difference is in their approach to life and how they might inspire others to make changes.

This leaves us with defining 'leadership'. Warren Bennis said, "Leadership is hard to define, but you know it when you see it." How true! We know it has something to do with people, but what is it exactly that leaders do? This quote from Norman Schwarzkopf is useful: "The challenge of leadership is to get people, willingly, to do more than they would, to rise above the norm, to perform at their higher level of potential." The key to this quote is the word 'willingly'. Leaders don't need a stick in the cupboard to force and threaten people to do things, and they support people to take that step beyond their comfort zone. As Warren Bennis also said in 'Learning to Lead': "The basis of leadership is the capacity of the leader to change the mindset, the framework of another person."

Here are some more definitions that provide other perspectives:

"Leadership is a function of knowing yourself, having a vision that is well communicated, building trust among colleagues, and taking effective action to realise your own leadership potential."

Warren Bennis & Robert Townsend: 'Reinventing Leadership' 1995

"The most effective leaders, political or corporate, empower others to act – and grow – in support of a cause that both leaders and followers find worthy. The leader's job is at once to articulate the empowering vision, and to stay in touch with followers to ensure that she or he is in tune with the needs of the real world where the vision is implemented."

Tom Peters: 'Thriving on Chaos' 1987

"There is no substitute for leadership. But management cannot create leaders. It can only create the conditions under which potential leadership qualities become effective; or it can stifle potential leadership."

Peter Drucker: 'The Practice of Management' 1954

"Leadership is about change, about taking an organisation or a group of people from where they are now to where they need to be."

Noel M. Tichy: 'The Leadership Engine' 1997

A Brief History of Leadership

Views of leadership are changing constantly. Thinking historically, leaders that stand out are usually strong military people, who achieved outstanding success in leading troops on the battlefield, such as Caesar, or Nelson or perhaps achieving success against the odds with strength of character, such as Elizabeth I. Alternatively, they were leaders in their field of discovery or innovation, such as Da Vinci or Galileo. It is not until around the 19th Century that we start to see more about leaders known also for their softer people skills, such as Florence Nightingale. Political leadership also starts coming to the fore.

In the 20th Century, we continued and expanded our requirement for true leaders as being those who not only have a strength of vision and the ability to put that across, but also those who have (or had) a true respect and interest in people. Nelson Mandela and Mother Teresa are examples here. In the industrial field, figures like Richard Branson featured (and still do feature) constantly for their people skills and outstanding success.

In the 21st Century, people's view of the leader is still changing. Leaders are sought closer to home in local communities where they can be seen as role models. The new leader is always learning and instilling a love of learning in others, as Peter Senge says in 'The Fifth Discipline': "The new view of leadership in learning organisations centres on subtler and more important tasks. In a learning organisation, leaders are designers, stewards and teachers. They are responsible for building organisations where people continually expand their capabilities to understand complexity, clarify vision, and improve shared mental models – that is, they are responsible for learning."

So is leadership about power, character, personality, behaviour, charisma or influence? In the business or corporate world, is it only true that you are a leader (of whatever description) if you have the word leader in your job title? Not necessarily.

My perspective is to suggest that leadership is a position of influence, to engage and involve people to move forward. I invite you to consider your perspective on leadership from the point of view of opportunities that exist to lead.

Leadership opportunities exist beyond the workplace, into all aspects of life – e.g. leadership in the community, in sport, at home, in religion, politics and developing/pioneering new ideas and concepts.

I would also like to invite you to challenge a common assumption that to be a leader you need a team of direct reports. It may be the case that because of having the responsibility for a team of people, you are deemed a leader – the title 'leader' may or may not be in your job title – but are you in fact acting as leader?

I would like to propose that a leader is a person who has followers, regardless of their title and responsibilities. And a follower is someone who buys into your vision and direction, willingly and with confidence in your leadership. They are inspired by you to generate new ideas and take responsibility for making them happen.

Getting the most from this book

This book is not about creating the ultimate 21st Century definition on leadership. It is about challenging and encouraging you to think about how you can make a difference as a leader in a straightforward and practical way.

This book also introduces the ThinkOn® system at a personal and organisational level to help you develop your leadership thinking.

This book is designed to explore some of the differences between managers and leaders. It is divided into sections each headed up with a thought provoker which becomes the thinking theme for that section. For each thought provoker you will find a load of tips around the key principles of the ThinkOn® system. I've also given some suggested listening for you by recommending episodes from our successful podcast series 'Thinking For Business Success', which can be downloaded free from iTunes. Each section closes with questions to develop your thinking in order to take action and measure your results.

To get the most from this book I encourage you to write in it, highlight your favourite bits, open it often and dip into it when you are in need of inspiration and new ideas. If you are serious about making a difference you will get most value by completing the 'Take Action' exercise in each section.

Remember that being a leader is influencing the thinking of others, so how about making use of the offer at the back of the book and sharing this resource with others?

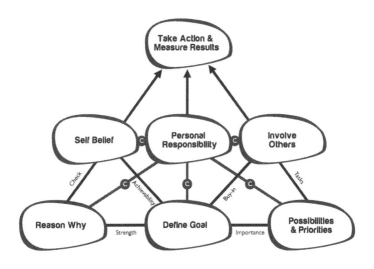

The ThinkOn® Results Framework

Because it is a system, it is important to pay attention to all principles and the connections between them. By doing this you will create a set of actions that will lead you to the results you desire, more creatively, consistently and efficiently.

At a personal level, you can use the principles within the thinking system to develop yourself as a leader. Before you get into the detail of the differences between managing and leading, start by answering these questions:

Define Goal

Specifically what kind of leader do I want to be?

How will I measure my leadership ability?

When do I want to be a better leader than I am today?

Reason Why

How important is it for me to develop as a leader?

What is my motivation for being a leader?

How serious am I about developing my leadership?

Self Belief

How confident am I that I can be the kind of leader that I want to be?

How could I build my confidence as a leader?

What helpful thoughts could I develop to build my self-belief as a leader?

Possibilities & Priorities

What might get in the way of my leadership development?

What possible things could I do to develop myself?

What priority actions do I need to take?

Involve Others

Who could possibly help me to become a better leader?

What possible advice could I get from a leader I admire?

How could I possibly get the buy-in of others to help me to develop my leadership skills?

Personal Responsibility

How much time will I choose to spend on my own leadership development?

What choices do I need to make to further my own development?

When will I plan in time to develop myself?

Take Action & Measure Results

What is my first step?

When will I start?

How will I track my own progress along the way?

Answering these questions will help to focus your mind as you read through the rest of this book.

If you want to understand more about the ThinkOn® Results Framework and how it can be applied to increase your own personal effectiveness in any situation, I recommend you read 'The Art of Making A Difference'.

Leadership Team Thinking

So far I have introduced you to a way that you can develop your leadership thinking at an individual level. Now I will introduce you to the ThinkOn® Leadership Framework which is a powerful thinking system for leadership teams in organisations. The Leadership Framework is an adaptation of the original ThinkOn® system and therefore has a direct read across to the original principles and links.

Take Action & Measure Results

ThinkOn® Leadership Framework

To help your leadership team with their thinking when planning or reviewing vision, strategy or change, here are a set of really useful questions based around the Leadership Framework, that if answered will increase your probability of success. The key to these is to answer them as a leadership team – this will give you opportunity to surface different perspectives and create an aligned team.

At the heart of the Leadership Framework is **Leadership Responsibility.** When using this model I recommend you start your thinking with this principle – if a strategy or change is going to be successfully implemented it is going to be the responsibility of the leadership team to put in place the infrastructure, processes and enablers, to manage both the task of change and people side of transition.

- What does leadership responsibility mean in this organisation and in the context of this change?

- How will we tangibly know when we are demonstrating leadership responsibility?

- What do we need to adopt or change in our behaviours as a leadership team to demonstrate a strong unified approach?

- How will we work as a leadership team to help the organisation and each other move towards the goal?

- Are we prepared to take full responsibility for role modelling the style of leadership we wish to see in this organisation that will contribute to us achieving our results?

Once you have absolute clarity on the Leadership Responsibility then as a leadership team you can ask questions based on the other five principles to help collectively develop your leadership thinking.

Organisational Reason Why – this will stimulate your thinking around the internal and external drivers and motivators for change. Internal drivers might include rising costs, poor workforce engagement, slow product innovation, restructuring, the need to replace out of date processes and equipment. External drivers might include global economic conditions, exchange rate fluctuations, increased competitor activity, legislative changes that require a different way of working, technological advances and environmental standards.

- What are the organisation's reasons for us adopting this strategy?
- What is the strongest reason for this?
- On a scale of 1 to 10 how passionate are we as a leadership team about bringing this strategy to fruition?
- Where would this rank amongst our other priorities on a 'reason why' scale?
- What processes could we put in place to check the strength of our organisational reason why, both at a leadership team level and at employee level?

Vision and Objectives – this principle allows you to test whether the organisational vision and objectives are expressed with absolute clarity and consistency and that the relevant people are able to describe it and buy into it. In my experience it is not unusual for a set of individuals who make up a leadership team to have contrasting views on the vision and its time scale. This difference of opinion will have a knock on effect all the way down through the organisation.

- What is the leadership vision for this organisation?
- How could we visibly communicate a consistent and aligned approach to the vision and objectives?
- How could we get clarity on exactly what it is we are going to do and by when?
- On a scale of 1 to 10 how achievable do we believe the vision to be?
- What steps could we put in place as we progress, to ensure we are still aligned and consistent, and to check the vision and objectives are still relevant and achievable?

Culture – every individual holds a set of beliefs about themselves and their workplace. Those beliefs may be unchallenged assumptions and not necessarily facts and they may be engrained having been formed over many years. Regardless of the origin and validity of those beliefs, people will act in accordance with them. An organisational culture is the collective sum of all your employees' beliefs, which can of course be either helpful or hindering towards the organisation achieving its goals.

- How strong is the existing culture to support the vision?

- What will need to change and what will stay the same?

- How could we possibly champion, reward and role model the culture required, for us to achieve the results we need?

- What hindering thoughts do we have as a team that impact on our confidence to implement our vision and what would be a more helpful thinking approach?

- How will we measure the culture shift?

- How could we organisationally celebrate the small wins and successes along the way to help build the organisation's belief and confidence?

Management Thinking and Planning – this explores what management activity needs to take place to achieve the vision. This includes thinking about how much time managers are able to give to the achievement of the vision and to what extent their activities are in line with the organisational goal.

- How could we develop and equip managers with the style and skills to help their teams achieve their goals?

- How much individual attention are we prepared to give ourselves to support those managers in their own leadership development?

- As a leadership team how could we challenge ourselves to do things differently, to release or create time for managers to enable them to focus on delivering the vision?

- How could we possibly communicate the vision and objectives to this population so that they have absolute clarity on their priorities and buy-in to the organisation's goal?
- What could we do as a leadership team to develop solution focused thinking habits in this population?

People – paying attention to this principle will widen your leadership team's thinking around the range of people who need to be engaged and bought into the organisational goal, and the different strategies that might be required to involve them. This could include thinking about how you might segment employees into different 'consumer groups' who may require different types and frequency of communication. For example, in your organisation there might be different leadership groups, different functional groups, and representative bodies such as the Trade Union.

As well as employees you could consider customers, shareholders, suppliers and other strategic partners or alliances.

- Who are the different people (either individuals or groups) that we need to communicate to and by when?
- How could we possibly communicate our vision in different ways to different groups so that it is impactful and captures both hearts and minds?
- What responsibility will we take to ensure the strategy or vision is communicated to others?
- How could we possibly identify what people want to know? How might we possibly establish how people want to receive information?
- Where and how could we get people involved at various stages of the organisation's journey to success so that people feel involved and informed?

Take Action and Measure Results – using the Leadership Framework is not a one-off event. Make it part of your implementation and review processes as a diagnostic tool. Determine which principle needs the greatest attention and then act on it.

> ## Thought Provoker
>
> Managers develop the steps and establish plans;
> Leaders develop the vision and establish direction.

What is the point of having a vision if no one knows about it, understands what it means for them and can't see your passion for it? Imagine Martin Luther King delivering his 'I have a dream speech' with no passion in his voice. How many people would he have been able to motivate?

Tips and Ideas

Define Goal

1.   Focus on the common goal.

2.   Create a compelling vision by presenting a picture of the future that is not only clear, but catches people's attention.

3.   Be willing to review the vision and change course if necessary, but let your people know the reason why.

4.   Ensure the new vision is visible in the workplace by aligning management processes and style with the values and behaviour implied.

5.   Develop your artistic ability! You need to paint vivid pictures of your vision of the future for your team to see.

6.   Develop long-range perspective.

7.   To be a leader you need vision. Vision is about seeing more than just what is in front of you, it's about imagining what could be.

8.   Be results-orientated.

9.   Create the vision and the long-term goals; allow others to create procedure and applications.

10. Develop your linguistic ability and communicate your vision to appeal to different senses:

> Visual – what does it look like?
> Auditory – what does it sound like?
> Kinaesthetic – what does it feel like?

11. Focus on the outcome desired rather than the path taken.

Reason Why

12. Make it absolutely crystal clear to everybody in your organisation what you stand for, what you value and what the big picture is.

13. Test your vision out on others. If you have to read it, it won't be inspiring. If you relay it verbatim, it won't convey your passion. Tell people what it means to you and to them – the reason why it's so important – and notice the difference!

14. Be passionate about your objective. One of the best ways to inspire others is to be motivated and enthusiastic yourself. High levels of passion and enthusiasm are contagious and will be the driving force to achieving the objective when things get tough.

15. Answer the question, 'Why would I want to come your way?' before someone else asks this question of you.

Self Belief

16. Let go of the past and focus on the future.

17. Believe in what you say and say what you believe.

Possibilities & Priorities

18. Plan in time to think. Thinking time is essential if you want your vision to become reality.

19. Develop a plan that gives everyone in the organisation absolute clarity about what their role is in contributing to the vision being achieved.

20. Explore all the possible ways that you could communicate and get the buy-in to the vision:

    - What if there was no PowerPoint?

    - How could you make communication two-way?

    - How could you show that you've listened to feedback?

Involve Others

21. Share with people what you want to be achieved rather than telling them how to achieve it.

22. Align people and communicate the direction through words and deeds.

23. Consider who could help and inspire you to create the vision.

24. Identify those whose involvement will add passion, focus, clarity and creativity to the vision.

25. Align the team around the vision and the values and get buy-in from everyone to move forward on those standards and behaviours.

26. Ensure managers understand and have bought into your vision. Give them a strong reason why, make it relevant to them and reward them for their successes.

27. Identify 'allies' to help take a vision forward.

28. Take time to understand those you want to inspire and what you need to do to make your vision real to them.

Personal Responsibility

29. Put aside sufficient time to 'scan the horizon' to check that the vision fits, is still relevant and that you are still on course to achieve it.

30. Think about how you can help others to feel willing and able to take personal responsibility for making the vision come to life.

Time to Take Action & Measure Results

Complete this table to define three goals to take action on:

Goal No.	What specifically will you achieve?	By when? (date?)	Success Measure
1.			
2.			
3.			

Who will I involve to help me achieve these goals?

How and when will I measure my progress?

What reflections have I had about myself?

Thought Provoker

Managers administer; Leaders innovate.

This is all about creating possibilities and new thinking. A leader will be stretching not only their own imagination but the imagination of those all around them to discover new ways of doing things. This reminds me of the quote from Oliver Wendell Holmes "A mind stretched to new ideas never returns to its original dimensions."

Tips and Ideas

Define Goal

31. Define some goals about being innovative – where in your working week are there opportunities for new and different thinking?

32. Set some measures and targets for innovation, both for yourself and for the organisation.

33. Plan a creative way of working into every day.

34. Ask yourself the question – 'What does creativity mean to me?'

35. Identify at what times of the day you are most creative and ring fence that time on a regular basis.

Reason Why

36. Ask, 'Why not' rather than 'Why'.

37. Create an environment that inspires and motivates people to come up with new and different thinking.

Self Belief

38. Have the courage to be different.

39. Create a thinking space in your mind and visit that place consciously at least once a day.

Possibilities & Priorities

40. Stretch your mind and take a risk – you never know what new opportunities might open up to you.

41. Take risks and accept the mistakes you will make as learning on the journey to far greater success.

42. Think outside the box. Keep making the box bigger.

43. Think inside the box – what could you do differently within the boundaries that you've been given?

44. Seek out different methods of working and problem solving. Read some development material on creative thinking.

45. Keep an ideas book to write down all your good ideas as they come to you. Regularly review your notes and assess what could be implemented for the good of the organisation.

46. Think possibilities – when thinking through actions to take consider as many options as possible. By doing this you will open your mind to new ways of doing things as opposed to the old tried and tested way.

47. Ask yourself questions that start with – 'What if' and 'Imagine if'.

Involve Others

48. Embrace and encourage flexibility and innovation, allowing others to follow your lead.

49. Go back to a 'childlike state' – let go of rules, social constraints, boundaries, self-limiting beliefs and assumptions – but without the tantrums and stamping of feet!

50. Generate an atmosphere that celebrates success and innovation with appropriate reward structures.

51. Seek out people who have a different perspective from yourself to help you think differently.

Personal Responsibility

52. Choose to let go of things that you no longer NEED to do.

53. Look for, create and take innovative opportunities to save or make your organisation money. Put forward robust business plans to introduce the improvements.

54. Identify ways in which to develop your creativity, such as identify a role model to learn from, read different books to your normal books, become skilled at possibility thinking – getting lots of ideas in a short space of time, go on a course, challenge your own thinking – engage your imagination, learn a new skill.

Time to Take Action & Measure Results

Complete this table to define three goals to take action on:

Goal No.	What specifically will you achieve?	By when? (date?)	Success Measure
1.			
2.			
3.			

Who will I involve to help me achieve these goals?

How and when will I measure my progress?

What reflections have I had about myself?

Thought Provoker

Managers focus on systems and structure;
Leaders focus on people.

Leadership is primarily about people. The quote from Peter Senge in the Introduction also talks about learning. Encouraging people to learn and grow provides one of the main motivational factors for people today, one that will ensure that you have the best people working for you, as well as guaranteeing that they will give you loyalty. Not surprisingly this section has a lot of tips related to the Involve Others principle in the ThinkOn® system and in my experience involving others is often overlooked or taken for granted. As with a lot of the tips in this book they are simple common sense – but ask yourself how often is common sense common practice?

Tips and Ideas

Define Goal

55. Build your vision of the future by engaging the imagination of those who will live in that future.

56. Ask yourself, 'To what extent do people know what they contribute to this organisation?' and then take action yourself to ensure everyone has absolute clarity.

57. Define yourself goals to ensure you focus on people, such as how many times you will ask for input in a week, how many times you will celebrate the successes and the 'wins', and how much you have shown encouragement and support to people individually over the week.

58. Define yourself a goal about what kind of leader you want to be, by thinking about what kind of legacy you want to leave.

Reason Why

59. Work with those who are happy to keep going in the face of failure.

60. Understand the needs/wants/motivations of others.

61. Find out the real reasons why people do the things they do.

62. Explain the reasoning behind an unpopular decision in order to create adult relationships and foster creativity.

63. Ask yourself, 'How good is the morale in the team? What could I do to improve it?'

Self Belief

64. Think of all that unharnessed potential of the individual before their upbringing and schooling conditioned it out of them. How can you recapture that untapped potential?

65. Use helpful solution focused language to encourage a helpful solution focused response.

66. Energise people to overcome barriers.

67. Believe in the ability of the people around you and have faith in their intent.

68. Find out what they want or need to develop to improve themselves, and then give it to them.

69. Inspire confidence in those around you.

70. Encourage others to set their own personal and professional goals. Openly discuss and support them in their career aspirations and life goals in line with the needs of the business.

Possibilities & Priorities

71. Know that people will do things differently to the way that you may do them. Be prepared to consider all the possibilities.

72. Accept ideas from your team and allow them to make it reality.

Involve Others

73. Understand the psychology of transition, i.e. how people behave during change and you will become excellent at leading people through change.

74. Show that you do listen to the thoughts and ideas of others through demonstrable actions.

75. Believe in others' ability to achieve what is needed.

76. Engender a culture of openness by developing an appropriate style to suit individuals at all levels, and speak their language.

77. Talk to others.

78. Think about the individual rather than the job the individual does.

79. Empower the people who work in your team to encourage a personal responsibility culture.

80. Allow people the freedom to make mistakes and capture the relevant learning.

81. Coach and mentor your team to make a difference. This will ensure they are well positioned and motivated to make a difference in your business in whatever area you agree.

82. Problem solve by proxy. What do you want the team to learn? If we solve the problems, then the team learns that we solve the problems and they will continue to come to us with them. Coaching them to solve their own will release you to focus on other areas of leadership and allow them to own the solution.

83. Concentrate on your people and the bottom line will take care of itself.

84. Remember the bottom line isn't just about profit, it's about the people who help make that profit. Develop a variety of measures of success, including ones that focus on your people.

85. Use the knowledge of others around you.

86. Be approachable.

87. Influence the creation of teams for the greater organisational good.

88. Let other people 'lead' if they know better than you in that situation.

89. Say, 'Good morning' to your receptionist and your cleaner and engage them in conversation. They are as vital to the smooth running of your business as any other member of the team – and they'll love you for it.

90. Give your time and concern to others and they will return the compliment by putting themselves out for you when you need it.

91. To be a manager, rely on systems and structure. To be a leader, rely on your people.

92. Invest time in your people and the problems will become less expensive.

93. Become a gardener – grow your people and don't be afraid to move them around the plot!

94. Build your people to create your processes.

95. Make good customer service happen by engaging the people – not relying on the process.

96. Create the environment that allows people to make mistakes and trusts others to do their best without seeking permission.

97. Get your people's involvement and buy-in and give recognition for their contribution.

98. Uncover the hidden talents in others. Recognise each person's strengths and make the best use possible of those strengths. What unused skills could be put to use in the workplace?

99. Seek out the future talent of the business. Help others to develop beyond their current roles and be ready for the requirements of the future.

100. Focus on win/win situations with your people.

Personal Responsibility

101. Show an individual by role modelling rather than by telling.

102. Show people how their work is meaningful and contributes to worthwhile ends.

103. Be your own person – not a copy. Be authentic.

104. Commit to a language and ways that are meaningful to others.

105. Inconvenience yourself for the sake of your people where necessary to make it happen.

106. Back the decisions of others around you.

107. Banish blame.

108. Choose your team first and then set the direction.

109. Ask what you can do for others and then do it. Ask others what they think they can do for you.

110. Be consistent in your approach and the messages you give.

111. Become known as a people person through choosing to take actions consistent with this.

112. Choose and learn to inspire everyone in the organisation – develop an ability to inspire both the shop floor and at board level by talking their language.

113. Seek out people who inspire you and ask them to mentor you – use different mentors for different issues.

114. Allow the talent in your team to flow like a stream down a hill – let it find its own way down and you'll discover it's the best way.

115. Develop your followership skills as well as your leadership skills.

116. Discuss your expectations with your team members. What do they expect of you and what do you expect of them? What will taking personal responsibility mean in your team?

117. Ask yourself on a regular basis, 'How do people know that I care about them?'

118. Ask yourself, 'What is it REALLY like to be lead by me?'

Time to Take Action & Measure Results

Complete this table to define three goals to take action on:

Goal No.	What specifically will you achieve?	By when? (date?)	Success Measure
1.			
2.			
3.			

Who will I involve to help me achieve these goals?

How and when will I measure my progress?

What reflections have I had about myself?

Thought Provoker

Managers watch the bottom line;
Leaders scan the horizon.

Scanning the horizon requires an open mind. Often we become bogged down in the trivialities of everyday things and forget to take the time to look up and around us. The world is changing very quickly. Many leaders have experienced a downfall when they become complacent and have forgotten to scan the horizon to see what's going on in their organisations, in the market place and with their competition.

Tips and Ideas

Define Goal

119. Develop 360 degree vision.

120. Do some scenario planning and create some contingency goals.

Reason Why

121. Show you care about the goals, and the work your team does each day to achieve them.

Self Belief

122. Understand the 'givens' that are true.

Possibilities & Priorities

123. Have an open mind.

124. Explore possibilities, then explore some more.

125. Know your business from top to bottom. Identify the habits of successful leaders and test them for yourself. Then explore new ideas, new ways of doing things.

126. Identify new opportunities and changes in the market place. What will impact on the business and how can the business make the most of it?

127. Introduce regular discussion and sessions on how to move the business forward. What actions can be taken to keep ahead in the market? Keep abreast of the elements that will impact on your organisation. Plan this into your diary system to ensure it happens.

128. Plan in quality thinking time. Make time to allow yourself to think about trends and how they impact on your organisation. Make time to generate ideas on how latest thinking can be integrated into the business.

Involve Others

129. Actively LOOK for the successes of others and learn from them.

130. Know the competition.

131. Drive the future of your organisation by involving those whose futures you want to enrich.

132. Ask your people to imagine the perfect world and empower them to create it.

133. Live life in someone else's shoes.

134. Consider how you might possibly use all of your people to help scan the horizon.

135. Discover the trends amongst your customers and personally speak to them on a regular basis.

136. Ask yourself, 'When did I last actively talk to people not only in my department but also in other departments about the view from their perspective?'

Personal Responsibility

137. Develop an insatiable curiosity about the outside world. You just never know where the next good idea may come from.

138. Get out of your office and go on a walk about.

139. Allow the manager to construct the ladder – your job will be to make sure it is up against the right wall.

140. You have two ears and one mouth – use them in that proportion to generate vision for your people.

141. Take time to stick your head above the parapet to see what's going on around you.

Time to Take Action & Measure Results

Complete this table to define three goals to take action on:

Goal No.	What specifically will you achieve?	By when? (date?)	Success Measure
1.			
2.			
3.			

Who will I involve to help me achieve these goals?

How and when will I measure my progress?

What reflections have I had about myself?

Thought Provoker

Managers imitate; Leaders originate.

At first glance this appears very similar to the section about innovation. This section though, is not so much about creating new ways of doing things and creating new products, as just doing things differently. A new manager might make the assumption that just because that is the way things have always been done, that is the way he or she should continue doing them. A leader, however, will find out how things have been done before and ask the question 'What might be a better or more effective/more efficient way of doing this?' 'What if we were to change the way we did this?' and 'What would happen if we didn't do this at all?' Doing things differently requires a different mindset, and brings to mind the saying 'Doing what you've always done will always give what you've always got'. An analogy might be always driving the same way to work in the morning and complaining about how long it takes you, without ever thinking about how you could achieve the same thing in a different way, perhaps along a different route, with a faster car, going at a different time of day and so on. If you find yourself complaining about something so much that your reason why to change becomes really strong, then define your goal as to what exactly you want to achieve, and explore the alternative possibilities of how to get there.

Tips and Ideas

Define Goal

142. Challenge yourself to do at least one different thing each day.

143. Give yourself a motto for learning. How about this – 'Imagine it. Test it. Prove it. Do it.' Think of the results you might achieve.

144. Use different methods or techniques for defining goals – be original.

Reason Why

145. Question the reason why. Rather than imitate what has gone on before, ask yourself, how could I do something differently?

146. Examine your motivation for doing things. What has been a motivating factor might not be good enough when you do things differently.

Self Belief

147. Put yourself in a helpful frame of mind when you set goals and vision – this helps you to have more ideas.

148. Ask yourself what might happen if you changed your habits of a lifetime.

149. When you see people struggling with new ways, take immediate action to minimise any loss in their confidence.

150. Ask yourself, 'What are my personal unique selling points and how can I best display them?' All successful leaders have at least one USP they are remembered for.

Possibilities & Priorities

151. Set aside time to think.

152. Develop creative thinking. Introduce managers to a range of thinking techniques to improve their thinking ability. This could be facilitated through group sessions or self-managed learning.

153. Create possibilities.

154. Create a culture of risk taking. Allow managers to give things a go, introduce new concepts, allow failures and review learning.

155. Dispose of all processes and procedures that are not essential to the success of the business. This will help encourage individual thinking and creativity.

Involve Others

156. Be open and responsive to sharing knowledge – upwards as well as downwards. The people in your organisation have valuable ideas too.

157. Find someone who does well what you want to do and improve on it.

158. Gather as many new ideas and practices from other industries and sectors in order to break out of the mould of imitating.

159. Encourage a sense of social responsibility by supporting leadership participation in the community.

160. Present managers with new challenges. For example, involve them in developing a project from scratch, allowing ownership and creativity in achieving the end result.

161. Reward original ideas. Investigate if managers are encouraged to follow tried and tested paths or whether managers are rewarded for introducing new concepts.

162. Have an 'out of body experience'! Look at the situation from above or from the point of view of another person, and see what new insights it gives you.

163. Share your 'wins' with others, let everyone be successful.

164. Acknowledge and consider others' suggestions no matter how bizarre or obscure they might seem at first.

Personal Responsibility

165. Create more leaders by being a leader yourself.

166. Expect sometimes to get a smack on the nose for what you originate – not everyone will appreciate your forward-looking attitude.

167. Display the behaviours that you want others to display.

168. Be yourself. Watch and learn from others, without attempting to be them.

169. Lead from the front; others will follow if they believe you know what you are doing.

170. Take ownership for what you do.

171. Give people responsibility for implementing their own ideas.

172. Ask yourself, 'What is going to be different tomorrow and am I ready to make it happen?'

173. Ask yourself, 'Am I more concerned with winning the argument or finding the right solution?'

174. Take ownership of identifying opportunities.

Time to Take Action & Measure Results

Complete this table to define three goals to take action on:

Goal No.	What specifically will you achieve?	By when? (date?)	Success Measure
1.			
2.			
3.			

Who will I involve to help me achieve these goals?

How and when will I measure my progress?

What reflections have I had about myself?

Thought Provoker

Managers rely on control; Leaders inspire trust.

One of the most vital connecting lines in the ThinkOn® system is the one connecting 'Involve Others' with 'Define Goal', which is about obtaining buy-in from those whom you want to involve. Trust is a vital element that makes teams and change work, and without it a leader is doomed (witness the gradual downfall of any political leader that starts to happen when we begin to lose trust in him or her). It is also a vital element in communication. Where trust is present, people will believe that communication is open, honest and will make allowances if for some reason they are not informed. With exactly the same communication system, another set of people will complain about poor communication, claiming that they are only told what the top management want them to hear and that generally communication is lousy. The difference? In the second example, the top person has not inspired trust.

Tips and Ideas

Define Goal

175. A big question here is how will you determine how and when people trust you? It's not as simple as asking, 'Do you trust me?' which is a very challenging question for people to answer honestly. So identify a set of possible measures to assess whether people do actually trust you.

176. Let people know what your goal is – trust them to find the way there.

Reason Why

177. Let your people know the reason why, in a language that makes sense to the hearer and obtains their buy-in.

178. Know that people these days will question those in charge.

179. Explain the reasons underpinning decisions.

180. Display passion about the organisation/business.

181. Inspire trust by being consistent with your values and your team will soar. Rely on control and you will be the limiting factor in what your team can achieve.

182. Assess and understand what motivates each individual that you work with. How can you use this information to provide some external motivation?

183. Help individuals to take ownership of building a solution – get them to do it because they want to do it.

Self Belief

184. Recognise and praise the efforts and successes of others.

185. Give trust and you will encourage open, honest and helpful responses.

186. Showing trust gives people the sense of being valued, enabling them to grow and develop.

187. Celebrate the success of others.

188. Reward your team for their success, keep failure to yourself.

189. Turn negatives into positives. Ask yourself a high quality question about how to do it.

190. Create positive results through helpful open attitudes.

191. Be confident enough to ask for help when you need it.

Possibilities & Priorities

192. Breed dissatisfaction with the current position and satisfaction with continuous improvement.

193. Access your team's creativity through a climate of trust.

194. Involve Others

195. Change from telling others to inspiring others.

196. Delegate! Even when you believe you can do the job better yourself. How else will they get better at it?

197. Let people do things their way provided the results head in the right direction. Find yourself two sets of **OARS** to row your boat. You will require one set as a good manager to focus on:

> **O**utcomes
> **A**genda
> **R**ules and regulations
> **S**tructure.

198. You will require a second set of **OARS** as a good leader to focus on:

> **O**penness
> **A**cceptance
> **R**eliability
> **S**incerity.

199. Guide your team by enabling them to pull all the oars together. Encourage an environment where everyone in the team can confront problems and deal with them – and maybe not always involve you.

200. Make your team your extended family and treat them accordingly.

201. Allow people to make mistakes. Create the right environment for them to learn from their mistakes and develop.

202. Encourage your team to 'cross boundaries' to discuss issues and tasks without needing their line manager's authority. Encourage your people to 'publish' their thoughts and ideas for circulation and give them recognition.

203. Encourage others to become ambassadors to develop the culture and ethos of the company.

204. Give people the freedom to make their own decisions and they will take responsibility for their actions.

205. Ask your team what they need from you, rather than imposing on them what you think they need.

206. Encourage flexible working practice. Letting people have more control of their lifestyle will encourage the energies that think outside the box.

207. Work alongside grassroots staff for a minimum of three hours every month.

208. Trust your team to do their best, and they will surprise you by doing even better.

209. Trust your people to do their best and they will trust you to believe in their ideas.

210. Allow your team to express their ideas regarding changes that they can see need to happen.

211. Get to know work colleagues as people as well as their work persona. Take an interest in them on a personal level and show that you are genuinely concerned for their well being.

Personal Responsibility

212. First be trustworthy, i.e. be an example to the members of the team on standards and behaviours.

213. Act and behave in a way that is congruent with the values and vision of the business. People will notice if you don't and this will impact their behaviour.

214. Be accountable – and demonstrate it!

215. Remember that it takes years to build up trust, and it can be lost in an instant. It only takes suspicion, not proof, to destroy it.

216. Do what you say you are going to do.

217. Trust requires two parties – a giver and a receiver. Generate the latter by taking responsibility for doing the former.

218. Continually strive to achieve trust and maintain it.

219. Be seen to support the decisions of others.

220. Shut up and listen!

221. Be brave enough to say what you believe in.

222. Lead how you would like to be led.

223. Exercise forgiveness.

224. Make your life easy – give trust and reap the benefits of simpler routes to getting things done.

225. Become a good leader by understanding when and how to follow.

226. Lead your people and they will follow. Take control and you will lose leadership.

227. Do what you say you are going to do.

228. Be courageous. Ask if you don't understand, because someone will have the answer.

229. Ask yourself if your people are proud of working with you. There will be a direct link between the proportion of these people you have and the success you achieve.

230. Behave professionally at all times. Do what you say you are going to do and keep confidences at all times. Even when engaging at a personal level be aware of your position in the team.

231. Role model the behaviours you wish to see in others. Reward others for their behaviours as well as the tasks completed. It is important to live up to any standards that are agreed.

Time to Take Action & Measure Results

Complete this table to define three goals to take action on:

Goal No.	What specifically will you achieve?	By when? (date?)	Success Measure
1.			
2.			
3.			

Who will I involve to help me achieve these goals?

How and when will I measure my progress?

What reflections have I had about myself?

Thought Provoker

Managers accept the status quo;
Leaders challenge it.

Challenging the status quo is all about finding courage to act, determination to follow through and sometimes downright stubbornness to keep going when everyone seems to be against you. Some organisations are so bound by procedure, so weighed down by years of bureaucracy, that challenging the 'way we do things round here' can be a real uphill struggle. Many give up on the way, or become conditioned to stop questioning. Challenging the status quo can not only be risky, but it also brings with it a health warning! Challenging the way things are done may appear to you to be logical with the intention of improving efficiency, but many people might be seeing it as their job to operate the old system. Challenge the system, and it might be construed that you are working to take their jobs away. If this applies to you, then re-read the sections on 'People' and 'Trust'!

Tips and Ideas

Define Goal

232. Decide right now – what difference do you want to make in this organisation?

233. Start with yourself, before you start leading others. Clarity brings you focus. Use the focus to define your goal.

Reason Why

234. When you have decided what difference you want to make in an organisation, ask yourself, 'What is the reason for doing this? Is it worth challenging the status quo to achieve it?'

235. Develop an insatiable curiosity about everything and everyone around you.

236. Challenge inertia by providing a strong reason why.

237. Highlight the consequences of not changing such that it increases the motivation of people to change.

Self Belief

238. What possible assumptions or self-limiting beliefs might you be holding that means the status quo goes unchallenged?

239. Challenge the beliefs of others.

240. Go on! Ask the obvious question – everyone else will be thinking it.

Possibilities & Priorities

241. Always look for the possibilities when faced with challenges. Create possibilities. Then create more possibilities.

242. Ask questions that you really want the answers to.

243. Challenge one thing every day by asking, 'What is the reason for it being this way?' and suggest an improvement.

244. Question traditions and sacred cows in a respectful and helpful way – you are then more likely to get buy-in to any changes.

245. Take a step back from the situation and picture a blank sheet of paper. Write your own ideas down to address the issue.

246. Consider what possible obstacles there might be – how could you overcome them?

247. In challenging the status quo, consider the possible risks. How could you possibly mitigate those risks and who could help you with that?

248. Develop the skill of asking high quality questions to engage imagination and focus the mind.

249. Be prepared to be out of control (for some of the time).

250. Question everything, but with the aim of increasing your understanding.

251. View problems as a learning process. They are challenges to be achieved rather than obstacles to be avoided.

Involve Others

252. Surround yourself with people who will challenge you.

253. Ask, 'Who could you involve in making this difference?'

Personal Responsibility

254. If it seems unreasonable or unexplicable – challenge it!

255. Consider what choices you will have to make in challenging the status quo.

256. If it's in your comfort zone, don't do it – delegate!

257. Ask yourself, 'What could I choose to learn today that might help me challenge in the future?'

258. Give your organisation a health check using the principles of the ThinkOn® system – challenge the status quo.

Time to Take Action & Measure Results

Complete this table to define three goals to take action on:

Goal No.	What specifically will you achieve?	By when? (date?)	Success Measure
1.			
2.			
3.			

Who will I involve to help me achieve these goals?

How and when will I measure my progress?

What reflections have I had about myself?

Thought Provoker

Managers produce predictability;
Leaders produce change.

'The only thing that is certain in life is change'. How many times have you heard that? Being a leader will make the difference between being reactive to change, with the change perhaps not being the change you desire, or being proactive and making sure that the change that happens is what you wanted and planned. So where would you, personally, prefer to be – in the driving seat or in the passenger seat?

So this is the step after challenging the status quo – to follow through with producing real change for the better. Within the ThinkOn® system we have reached the top, taking action and measuring results. To produce change, the reason why has to be strong, the goal has to be clear and the self-belief has to be high to keep going in the face of adversity. An outstanding leader will have considered a wide-range of possibilities, prioritised them and involved others. Above all the leader takes personal responsibility for making the change happen.

Tips and Ideas

Define Goal

259. Decide where you would personally prefer to be in relation to change – in the driving seat or the passenger seat?

260. Develop goal-defining skills. Have short-term and long-term goals. Have personal and professionals goals. Use these goals to keep your focus on the things that are important to you.

261. Celebrate your wins. Set yourself daily or even hourly goals. Recognise when these goals are achieved and give yourself a reward or a pat on the back.

262. Measure success on a consistent basis, never be satisfied with 'it's good enough'. Always ask, 'How can it be improved?'

263. Ask yourself, 'What have I done to make a difference today?'

Reason Why

264. Balance 'away from' motivation with 'towards' motivation to create momentum and direction to your change.

Self Belief

265. What might be the thoughts that your team has that might hinder change? Find out what they are and then work with them to find solutions to their concern.

266. Keep learning. Seek to develop new skills and improve your current ability.

267. Look for the good things in any change.

268. Watch out for feelings of uncertainty, unfairness or powerlessness in others during change. Consider how you might help them minimise those feelings with information and involvement.

Possibilities & Priorities

269. Ask, 'What's the best thing that could happen, and what's the worst?'

270. Think to yourself, 'There's always a better way – I just have to find it!'

271. Be flexible – your way isn't any better or any worse than anybody else's – just different.

272. Embrace the unpredictability of exploring 'the new'.

273. Ask yourself, 'If you stop doing things in this way, or even if you stop doing them at all, would anyone notice or even care?'

274. Investigate alternative ways of undertaking one day-to-day task.

Involve Others

275. Spend quality time with your staff exploring new ways of working.

276. Surround yourself with people who are different to you.

277. Develop change as the norm. Encouraging your people to embrace change will be one way of keeping ahead of the competition.

278. Employ people who know more than you do.

279. Make a conscious effort to find different ways to involve people in change – even asking for their suggestions can make people feel they have had some involvement.

280. To bring out the best in people foster a relationship with them as a person.

Personal Responsibility

281. Be persistent – this is different to banging your head against a brick wall!

282. Make decisions quickly.

283. Think in a solution focused way. Develop clear goals for making a difference and use creative possibility thinking techniques to explore the parameters of what can be achieved.

284. Be able to change your mind about things for the right reasons.

285. Initiate personal change. Change your routine; change the way you travel to work; change what you have for lunch – anything to get you in the 'change' frame of mind.

286. Notice how you feel and what you say to yourself in change – take responsibility for any thoughts that are hindering and make a choice as to whether you want to change them.

Time to Take Action & Measure Results

Complete this table to define three goals to take action on:

Goal No.	What specifically will you achieve?	By when? (date?)	Success Measure
1.			
2.			
3.			

Who will I involve to help me achieve these goals?

How and when will I measure my progress?

What reflections have I had about myself?

Thoughts to finish with

Many of these tips are about taking personal responsibility for your own leadership, rather than relating specifically to the previous themed sections.

Tips and Ideas

287. Lead by example.

288. Be ready for the setbacks, but don't let it put you off. The harder you try, the luckier you'll get.

289. Remember you don't have to be a manager to be a leader and remember you can be a leader and a manager.

290. Buy your team a drink and celebrate success – it makes everyone feel good and more motivated.

291. Be prepared to get your hands dirty and do it yourself, otherwise you can't expect others to do it.

292. Choose to consider everyone as having leadership potential and take it upon yourself to find out what that potential is.

293. Communicate and live for what you value; reward and recognise others in the organisation who also live those values and deliver the goals.

294. Actively encourage the learning and development of others.

295. Have a banana and run up the stairs.
    (This one does require special explanation and you may have guessed that actually what we are saying is 'stay healthy'! It is proven that our brains do not need to degenerate with age, and two things everyone can do to help that process is to eat healthily and stay physically active. Leaders need to be able to think clearly and imaginatively, so an active brain is essential!)

296. Whether you act as a manager or a leader, you will be a role model for others. Act like a manager if you want more managers; act like a leader if you want more leaders.

297. Be proactive with your learning and development.

298. Be firm on ends, flexible on means. A leader is firm on the end goal, but does not need to be firm on how to get there. In fact, you will win more trust from your people if you allow them to decide on the means.

299. Be the one with the most energy, the most passion and the most commitment to the goals.

300. Lead from the front or the back. From the back you can allow the remainder of the team to drive the whole thing forward, which would be empowering. At the front you will demonstrate pace and speed and drive the momentum of the team to get things done.

301. The greatest thing a leader can do is to 'know thyself' before anything else.

302. A leader's greatest test of courage is to bear defeat without losing heart.

303. Ultimately a leader's job is to take people places they have never been before.

304. Continually develop your capabilities as a leader.

305. Good leaders will always allow the team to shine.

306. There is no recipe or formula for creating a leader. Dip in and out of many sources to create competence.

307. Managers that push boundaries and take risks eventually blossom into confident leaders.

308. Good leaders always play to their strengths and don't necessarily spend too long on their weaknesses.

309. Get people to generate ideas; some will be good and some not so good.

310. Build your people into good initiators and idea generators. Get their ideas and let them create!

311. Focus on the situation, issue or behaviour; do not make it personal.

312. Don't ask for opinions because you think you have to, ask for opinions because you want to and really listen to them (this will breed an inertia of ideas and thoughts through your own integrity).

313. Use your own travel time to think: planes, trains and automobiles are perfect times to be creative and plan new strategies.

314. Don't think you always have to tell them; ask them. Use open questions to discover opinions and ideas.

315. Go back to the floor; what do your people think you should do?

316. Don't rely on your board; ask your board to ask their people.

317. In a crisis, enable those involved to find solutions. Don't jump in and solve it for them.

318. Seek to employ people who challenge you.

319. Quiet people have a real impact too, so allow time for quiet people to reflect and give their ideas. Remember they may need time and options to express their ideas to you as a leader, they may not want to talk out loud to a big audience.

320. Behaviour breeds behaviour (so behave how you expect others to).

Well, now you have over 300 possibilities about transforming managers into leaders. Now it's up to you as to what difference you want to make in your leadership. The crux of the ThinkOn® system lies in the personal responsibility – quite simply, are you going to take personal responsibility to become a better leader or not?

Acknowledgements

We gratefully acknowledge the contribution of ideas from the following:

The ThinkOn team
Martin Alderman
Catherine Bottone
Thea Bredie
Gordon Brock
Chris Bulaitis
Colin Campbell
Marie-Claude Cavelier
Claire Davies
Alison Delchar
Glenn Dixon
Daniel Dohar
Shelley Edwards
Ann Fenton
Virginia Frazer
Natasha Goggin
Cathy Griffin
Neil Griffin
Vince Harvey
Andrew Ibbitson
Ray Jacobs
Steve Lavelle
Mike Leatt
Stephen Lehane
Judith Lyons
Jill Maycock
Esther O' Halloran
Steve Parker
Mike Rutter
Nancy Slessenger
Mike Smith
Bev Stephens
David Taeger
Nadine Taylor
Jeanette Wilkner

Suggested Reading

I asked the ThinkOn® team for their favourite books and films on leadership, together with an explanation of why they like them. I hope they will become your favourites too!

Nuts! – by Kevin and Jackie Freiberg
The story of South West Airlines, their challenging beginnings and how they have grown into America's wackiest and most successful airline. OK, so some of it seems over the top, but nevertheless it contains many easy to emulate ideas of what we can all do to be different. What I find really fascinating is their ability to retain the 'family' atmosphere with 23,000 employees. Quite a hefty book, but incredibly easy-to-read, beautifully presented, and easy-to-dip-into with its anecdotes and 'Success in a Nutshell' summaries.

The Spirit to Serve, Marriott's Way – by J.W. Marriott Jr. and Kathi Ann Brown
This book is the story of the rise of the Marriott Hotel chain written by the son of the founder. It is a very factual account of what they did, how important their values were, and difficult decisions they faced on the way. It is also an easy-to-read book about what made them leaders in their field.

First Break All The Rules – by Marcus Buckingham and Curt Coffmann
This book is based on research by the Gallup Organisation into what the world's greatest managers do differently. Actually, I would describe it as what managers do differently that transforms them into leaders. So much common sense that you wonder why it isn't common practice. Worth reading just for Chapter One, which explains the twelve questions that must be answered to measure the core elements needed to attract, focus and keep the most talented employees.

The Richer Way – How to Get the Best Out Of People – by Julian Richer
A very practical book full of straightforward common sense and advice about putting people – both staff and customers – right at the centre of a record breaking retail business that was started by a nineteen year old.

Leadership, The Never-Ending Story – by Paul Bridle
This book offers an easy-to-learn and easy-to-put-into-practice model of leadership that works. It is based on research carried out with people who work with outstanding leaders.

The Leadership Engine – by Noel M. Tichy
This is a rapid read handbook with lots of 'how to'. It focuses on leaders developing other leaders and is very practical.

Reinventing Leadership – by Warren Bennis & Robert Townsend
This book considers the techniques and strategies that constitute effective leadership with loads of exercises and questions – even a 21-Day Plan.

Leadership and the One Minute Manager – by Ken Blanchard
Very quick to read and very practical.

All Change – the Project Leader's Secret Handbook – by Eddie Obeng
Practical, gives lots of 'how to' and it's fun.

Zapp!: the Lightening of Empowerment – by William C. Byham
How to lead people to empowerment.

Ben & Jerry's Double Dip – by Ben Cohen and Jerry Greenfield
How to build and lead a 'values-led business'. Not just great ice-cream, but also great corporate social responsibility.

Losing My Virginity – by Richard Branson
A great inspirational, autobiographical adventure.

A Peacock in the Land of Penguins – by Barbara Hateley & Warren Schmidt
This is a fable about a peacock with much sought after talent and experience in his field. He is recruited into the corporate world of the land of penguins, because he is different and can bring in the experience they need. However, the reality is that whilst they say they value difference/diversity what they really want is conformity.

A great story on diversity in the workplace and leaders who say they want change but don't really mean it.

If you're not into reading books, how about these films instead:

Braveheart
The Scots did not have the self-belief that they could overcome the English. Watch how William Wallace gives them the self-belief through his inspiration, his values and through thinking differently.

Watership Down
The leader always puts himself forward for the sake of others and never leaves anyone behind.

One Flew Over the Cuckoo's Nest
Good fun and look how people followed. A great example of how to challenge the status quo.

Rob Roy
Rob Roy triumphs through being absolutely consistent with his values, even under pressure from his loved ones.

Chicken Run
Apart from being great fun, this is a brilliant example of instilling self-belief in others, working with people's strengths and creating perfect teamwork.

Dead Poets Society
Great lessons from an inspirational school teacher who challenges people to think and take responsibility for making the differences they want to make.

Discover More Ways To Make A Difference

You can find more books and online learning at www.gomadthinking.com or telephone +44 (0)1509 891313 to have a chat about developing yourself or your team.

The Art of Making A Difference
A great personal effectiveness book and an introduction to the ThinkOn® Results Framework.

Solution Focused Coaching
Over 200 powerful coaching questions, plus tips, tools, techniques and templates. The manager's guide for helping others to make a difference.

How to Save Time and Money by Managing Organisational Change Effectively
Essential information for managers to know and apply at time of change.

How to Save Time and Money by Managing Meetings Effectively
101 ways to make a difference before, during and after meetings.

If you are seeking to make a difference and would like to have a discussion about any aspect of management/leadership transformation, personal or business improvement or embedding solution focused thinking within your organisation, please contact us at:

Go M.A.D Ltd

Pocket Gate Farm

Off Breakback Road

Woodhouse Eaves

Leicestershire

LE12 8RS

United Kingdom

Tel: +44 (0) 1509 891313

E-mail: info@gomadthinking.com

NOTES/IDEAS

NOTES/IDEAS

NOTES/IDEAS

NOTES/IDEAS